How to A Document Control System based on ISO 9001:2015

Folarin Omojoye

Disclaimer

Please note that all definitions and illustrations expressed in this book are the views of the author. It does not represent the opinions of any entity whatsoever.

Methods favored as best practices in the past may quickly become obsolete as knowledge increases; hence readers must always rely on their own experience in analyzing and applying any information provided in this book.

The author, publisher, and anyone associated with writing this book shall not have any liability whatsoever for any losses, including losses for any omission, error, misinterpretation, or subsequent impact howsoever caused.

Dedication

Now all glory to God, who is able,
through his mighty power at
work within us, to accomplish
infinitely more than we might ask
or think.

Bible.

To Mmayen M. Pearls, my
patient wife.

Many thanks to you for enduring
many months while authoring this
book.

Table of Contents

Introduction

"For every operation audited, know the mission... the purpose... the reason for being," says Larry Sawyer.

So, what is the point of conducting a document control audit? What is the reasoning, mission, or goals?

- To check and strengthen document control practices especially where documentation issues have happened in the past or are imminent,

- To fulfill contract requirements or a request from a client or management team,

- To examine and evaluate the level of compliance to standards, requirements, laws, and procedures,

- To identify gaps in document control,

- To highlight the weakness and strength of the Document Control Department,

- It can be used as a basis for continuous improvement initiatives in document control,

- To get the organization ready for certification,

- To keep up with the latest developments and best practices in the industry,

- It can be used as a foundation for investor due diligence or take over of one firm from another,

- It can be used as a starting point for an electronic document management system implementation or a document control refurbishment project.

Auditing is a critical step in verifying that an organization's Quality Management System is working effectively.

Auditors, in particular, assess many elements of an organization's quality compliance effectiveness through the inspection of documented information whose audit trail is managed by document control.

Chapter 1: What is Document Control Audit and What Are the Different Types?

Document control audit is a system or compliance type audit.

- It is conducted to assess how well a company's document control system conforms to internal procedures as well as external regulations imposed on them.

- It may also be conducted to verify that the document control system follows industry best practices.

Note that the term "system" in this context does not necessarily refer to a computer system. It is an all-encompassing term for the auditable components of document control.

For example, we can check the numbering system, revision system, modifications control, transmittal rules, traceability, Electronic Document Management Software (EDMS), hardcopy cabinet, archival processes, and so on for compliance with the applicable audit criteria.

Apart from system audits, there are other types/forms of audits:

- **Product audit** - Audit conducted to examine a product's compliance to the product specification.

- **Process Audit** - Audit conducted to identify the inputs and outputs of a process and evaluate the controls to verify that the result is consistent.

- **Financial Audit** - Audit conducted to examine and evaluate an organization's financial statements to ensure that the financial records are a fair and accurate representation of the entity they purport to represent.

- **Information System Audit** - Audit that aims to provide an overview of the organization's information management systems to verify that they are functioning smoothly.

- **Best practices** - an audit that compares a company's practices to those of other firms that have been recognized as having exceptional practices.

Audits can also be classified based on who is conducting the audit, for example,

- **First-Party Audit** – audit undertaken by a company on its system. The goal is to determine if processes are followed and effective.

- **Second-Party Audit** - audit conducted by a company's client. They are based on a signed contract or predetermined conditions.

- **Third-Party Audit** - audit performed by an independent entity. The third party is not involved in the audited activity and it is based on predefined criteria.

Chapter 2: Glossary of Abbreviations and Terms

This chapter focuses on defining key terms and abbreviations.

Audit

A systematic, independent, and documented process for obtaining objective evidence and evaluating it objectively to determine the extent to which the audit criteria are fulfilled.

Audit criteria

Set of policies, procedures, or requirements that serve as a standard or reference against which objective evidence is compared.

Audit Evidence

Records, statements, or other information that are relevant to the audit criteria and verifiable.

Audit Findings

Results of the evaluation of the collected audit evidence against audit criteria.

Audit objective

The objective defines what is to be accomplished by the audit.

Audit Plan

Document describing the audit objectives, the scope, the criteria, the reference documents, the expected time and duration of the audits, the roles and responsibilities, the person to be interviewed, duration of the interviews. It may also contain other information such as logistics arrangement, confidentiality, the language of the audit, etc.

Audit Program / Schedule

Arrangement for a set of one or more audits planned for a specific time frame and directed towards a specific purpose.

Audit Report

Document containing the auditor's judgment on whether the audited entity is compliant with the audit criteria. It summarizes the locations, functions, processes audited, conformity / non-conformity items identified, and their supporting evidence. If applicable, it may also contain root cause, CA, PA, and SFI.

Audit scope

Extent and boundaries of an Audit. For example, the physical location, the organizational units, the activities, the processes, the time to be covered, etc.

Audit team

One or more persons conducting an audit, supported if needed by technical experts. The team is responsible for conducting the audit activities under Audit team leader.

Audit team leader

Person responsible for the smooth running of the Audit.

Audit Work Documents

Documents used for an audit, for example, checklists, which provide a list of important requirements to be checked, and forms for reporting or gathering evidence.

Auditee

Person or organization being audited. The auditee's responsibilities amongst others include:

- facilitating the availability of resources

- collaborating with the Audit Team to provide required information such as personnel information regarding the audit, representatives for interviews, up-to-date documents

- Managing logistical arrangements

- Assisting the audit team as needed in navigating the audited entity.

- Implementation of any preventive or corrective actions identified as a result of the audit.

Auditor

Person who conducts an audit.

Conformity

Fulfillment of a requirement.

Corrective Action (CA)

Action to eliminate the cause of a detected nonconformity or other undesirable situation.

Document control system

A Document Control System consists of the components of document control like the policy, parameters, elements, processes, technology, and strategy, etc.

Documented Information

Information required to be controlled and maintained by an organization and the medium on which it is contained.

Electronic Document Management System (EDMS)

EDMS is a generic term for any computer application used to store and manage electronic records, data, and documents.

Non conformance.

Non-fulfillment of a requirement.

Objective Evidence

Data, fact, etc. supporting the existence or verity of something

Observer

Person who accompanies the audit team but does not act as an auditor. The Observer can be a member of the auditee, a regulator, or other interested parties.

Observation

A statement based on a signal (*something one has seen, heard, or noticed*) for which additional information is required.

Preventive Action (PA)

Action to eliminate the cause of a potential nonconformity or other potential undesirable situation.

Quality management System (QMS)

The set of interrelated quality elements (policies, processes, and procedures) with which an organization can meet customers' and other applicable requirements consistently.

Suggestion for Improvement (SFI)

Suggestion that identifies areas for improvement in the audited entity.

Technical Expert

Person who provides specific knowledge or expertise to the Audit team.

Chapter 3: Benefits of Document Control Audit

The following are some of the ways that a document control audit will benefit your organization strategically, operationally, and administratively:

- It takes document control from being viewed only from the execution or implementation side of the organization's strategy to the business player side. If the organization's EDMS is being audited, for example, the auditor may request proof of EDMS requirement inputs from the document control department, as well as proof of Document Controller training for the needed competencies.

- It will help to clarify document control roles, duties, performance levels, professionalism, and effect on the company's strategic objectives.

- It will help to ensure that document control practices align with legal, contractual, standard, or customer requirements.

- It can reveal facts and information that may indicate where improvements are required. For example, which department is underperforming as measured by the percentage of documents rejected by clients owing to quality issues?

- It can reveal facts and information that may indicate where improvements are required. For example, which department is underperforming as measured by the percentage of documents rejected by clients owing to quality issues?

- In some cases, the audit may even save the company from documentation issues that could have resulted in significant financial consequences or litigation.

Chapter 4: Principles of a Document Control Audit

Auditors often find themselves balancing between two seemingly opposing positions: Observing best practices and identifying gaps. Finding a balance within these postures necessitates a thorough understanding of the fundamental audit principles outlined below.

- **Independenc**e – this implies that the auditors must not have had any involvement with the auditing system to avoid a conflict of interest. A document controller, for example, cannot audit its work. It has to be someone else.

- **Objective and Unbiased**- That is, the Auditors must report their findings in a way that is objective, verifiable, and unbiased. Auditors should not exhibit partiality and should refrain from expressing personal judgments.

- **Evidence-based** – The Audit report must be factual and accurate, with references to particular audit evidence, and must be performed on samples. For example, the audit report may have it that:

- ○ "Superseded documents are suitably identified and controlled. Some of the document seen with superseded stamped are x, y, z"

- ○ "Email workflow shows that project engineers receive document directly from subcontractor contrary to the requirements in Document control Procedure which says that all Subcontractor's document shall be received by the document controller for distribution to related department."

- **Ethical** - Auditors must be trustworthy and dependable, and they must approach their work with honesty, secrecy, and discretion.

- **Professionalism** –The Auditor should plan ahead of time, appear early, possess good communication skills, polite, and use the actual terms from the standards and procedures.

- **Process Focus** – The auditor is not looking to blackmail or unearth nonconformities. Rather, he or she must view the audit as a means of revealing best practices. As a result, the emphasis should be on processes rather than the Document Controller.

Chapter 5: Sources of Document Control Audit Criteria

As previously established, audit criteria are the references against which the conformance or otherwise of the audited company will be assessed.

The source of a document control audit criteria will vary depending on the kind of audit. The main sources are:

NATIONAL AND INTERNATIONAL INSTITUTIONS – Requirements from organizations that have been acknowledged, approved, and trusted with the development of Standards and Codes. For example, The International Organizations for Standardization (ISO),

YOUR COMPANY POLICIES OR PROCEDURES - Standards that represent your organization's particular documentation goals and objectives.

CLIENT REQUIREMENTS - Client specifications. For example, a Contractor may be required to follow the client's numbering and revision system, templates, and so on.

STATUTORY AND REGULATORY BODIES - These are bodies established by legislation in a particular country. E.g. The Food and Drug Administration (FDA) of the United States, as well as the Canadian Quality Assurance and Control Standards. Failure to follow regulations may result in the loss of business or the revocation of the company's license to operate in that country.

Chapter 6: Audit checks based on the ISO 9001:2015 Clause 7.5

Our Audit check will be based on the ISO 9001:2015 standard requirements - the world's most famous quality standard for document control.

But first, what is ISO?

ISO (the International Organization for Standardization) is an independent, non-governmental, and global federation of national standards agencies.

ISO QUICK FACTS:

- ISO is not an abbreviation or acronym. It is a Greek term that means equal.

- It's headquarter is located in Geneva, Switzerland

- Established in February 23, 1947

- Mission: International Standards

- Website: www.iso.org

- Individuals or businesses cannot become ISO members.

- Each country has just one member in ISO who represents the foremost   standard-setting organization in that country.

- ISO group their frameworks into families. For example, ISO 14000 is the family of environmental management standards established to help organizations improve their environmental management performance, whereas ISO 9001 is the family of ISO standards that deals with an organization's quality management system.

- The ISO 9001 is often used as the Audit criteria to audit the company's document control system.

- The current edition as of the time of writing is ISO 9001:2015. The penultimate edition is ISO 9001:2008.

Following our understanding of ISO, we will now look at how to audit an organization's document control system using ISO 9001:2015 requirements as the audit criteria.

Note: You will find in **Appendix A,** the ISO 9001:2008 Section 4.2.3 requirements for the Control of documents.

Checking Document Control Compliance against the ISO 9001:2015 Section 7.5 requirements for the Documented Information.

REQUIREMENTS	ELEMENTS TO INVESTIGATE
7.5.2 Creating and updating **When creating and updating documented information, the organization shall ensure appropriate:**	
a) identification and description (e.g. a title, date, author, or reference number);	Look for procedures documenting the document numbering convention. Check for evidence that the document numbering convention is used as stated. Look for document templates showing the name or logo of the originating company, the document author, document title, document identification number, revision, revision date, etc.
b) format (e.g. language, software version, graphics) and media (e.g. paper, electronic);	These requirements are organization-specific. So check for evidence that the organization's specific rules for document format and media are followed as stated in the guiding procedure
c) review and approval for suitability and adequacy.	Check for flow charts or procedures showing a review or check process before the official issuance of documents. Check to see if the flowchart is being followed in practice. For example, look for an

	audit trail of review workflow in an EDMS that occurs before document publication or signatures of the Checker and Approver on official revisions of documents.

7.5.3 Control of documented information

7.5.3.1: Documented information required by the quality management system and by this International Standard shall be controlled to ensure:

a) it is available and suitable for use, where and when it is needed;	Look for distribution matrix and proof of correct implementation of distribution. Check that there is no discrepancy of revisions for the same document between the Home Office, site, the factory, and so on.
b) it is adequately protected (e.g. from loss of confidentiality, improper use, or loss of integrity).	Investigate the use of security access schemes that allow only authorized individuals to access classified information. Check for a controlled document distribution matrix. Check to see if consistent quality checks are performed in documents.

7.5.3.2 For the control of documented information, the organization shall address the following activities, as applicable:

a) distribution, access, retrieval and use;	Check for the existence of a department or person responsible for document distribution, access control, and administration of documents. Investigate the

	use of security access schemes for documented information.
b) storage and preservation, including preservation of legibility;	Look for evidence that the current revision and other revisions are stored correctly in the EDMS, Controlled Server, or the physical document storage facilities as applicable. Check for the archiving and preservation procedures and finally look for a checklist for quality checks.
c) control of changes (e.g. version control);	Look for procedures documenting the revision system and evidence that the revision system is followed consistently. Investigate that the current revision of documents can be distinguished from the obsolete documents. Look for annotation marks or highlights (such as clouds, or tracked changes, etc.) in documents from one revision to another.
d) retention and disposition.	Check for the existence of retention and disposal plans/schedules. Confirm this is by checking the revision dates of document samples against the schedule.
Documented information of external origin determined by the organization to be	Check for document control Instruction to contractors/vendors (if applicable) Look for templates for external

necessary for the planning and operation of the quality management system shall be identified as appropriate, and be controlled.	documents that indicate both the originating company's and of the client company's name or logo. Look for a distribution matrix showing a controlled distribution for this external document.
Documented information retained as evidence of conformity shall be protected from unintended alterations.	Look for obsolete revisions that have been relocated to an absolute folder with limited access, or watermarks or stamps on obsolete documents and revisions, or proof of measures that cannot be misunderstood by Users.

Chapter 7: Approach to a Document Control Audit

Let us now go through the various phases and processes of the Audit.

Preparation

- The responsible authority appoints the audit team leader and the audit team based on the required knowledge and skills.

- The team leader assigns work to the audit team and with the cooperation of the team,

    - Gather all the necessary information concerning the last Audits in the area involved (if any),

    - Write the heads of understanding and the audit work documents

    - Prepare, review and get the necessary approval for the audit plan,

Communication - Although communication is not an audit phase, nonetheless, it is an important step in the audit that brings together the various entities. Poor communication often creates some of the recurrent audit challenges. It is either the audit plan is not fully communicated, read, or agreed with the auditee. In some cases, they are completely ignored or not communicated to all the relevant parties involved. So, the audit team must;

- Establish an appropriate channel of communication from the start to determine the feasibility of the audit

- Give sufficient advanced notice so that the audit team and auditee may prepare the relevant information

- Explain the purpose, objectives, methodology, and scope of the audit,

- Provide information on timing, team composition, arrangements for the audit,

It should be noted that the Auditee has the authority to request the replacement of an Audit member on reasonable grounds. For instance, in the event of a conflict of interest.

Opening meeting

The audit activities start with the opening meeting having in attendance the audit team and auditee. The objectives of the opening meeting are:

- To formally introduce the audit team members and auditee

- To review the objective, the scope, and the criteria of the audit

- To clarify any other detail possibly from the auditee

On-Site Activities – During this phase, the Audit team will conduct interviews and, if necessary, field/site visits. The goal of the interviews and site visits is to gather objective evidence that will assist the audit team in justifying all audit findings.

Step 1 – Gather information (evidence) through interviews, observation of activities, documents (policy, procedure), and records. See Appendix B.

Step 2 – Analyze, investigate and verify each piece of the evidence against the audit criteria. These activities will lead to a list of audit findings.

Note:

Instead of investigating all the documentation, conduct checks on samples. The sample should be comprehensive enough to be representative of the entire system. If you discover one or more flaws, you can move on to additional targeting sampling to seek further evidence.

Step 3 - Record the list of audit findings (conformities, non-conformance, areas of improvement, etc.)

Step 4 – Conclude the audit:

- Review the audit findings against the audit objectives

- Assess the extent of conformity of the document control system with the criteria

- Write the recommendations for improvement.

Closing Meeting

At the end of the audit, a closing meeting is organized. It includes the audit team, the auditee and may also include other parties such as middle and top managers.

The meeting aims to present the audit findings and conclusions to ensure that they are understood and acknowledged by the audited entity. This activity is necessary to avoid post-audit disagreement.

Unresolved issues should be documented as well.

Reporting

Writing the Audit Report is the next major step. The Team Leader, with the assistance of his Team, decides which findings to include in the report. Ideally, the report will include the following information:

- Audit objectives and Scope

- Identification of the audit client

- Identification of the audit team

- Dates and location where on-site activities were concluded

- Audit criteria

- Audit findings

- Audit conclusions

- Audit recommendations and agreed follow-up action plan (if any)

Follow-up and Close-Out

There will be follow-up meetings after the Audit. The goal is to close out all the non-conformity items in the audit report.

It is important to note that the audit can only be considered closed once all corrective action has been implemented, verified, and the root cause has been addressed.

Appendix A: Section 4.2.3 Control of Documents (excerpts from ISO 9001:2008)

ISO 9001:2008 clause in terms of document control requires organizations to define controls needed to

a. Approve documents for adequacy prior to issue

b. Review, update, and re-approve documents, as necessary

c. Ensure that changes and the current revision status of documents are identified

d. Ensure that relevant versions of applicable documents are available at points of use

e. Ensure that documents remain legible and readily identifiable

f. Ensure that documents of external origin are identified and their distribution controlled

g. Prevent the unintended use of obsolete documents, and to apply suitable identification to them if they are retained for any purpose

Appendix B: Framework for Document Control Audit Interview Questions

Concentrate of the elements of the document control system such as the;

- The numbering system,

- The review and approval process

- The modifications control,

- Transmittal process,

- Traceability parameters/tools (revision code, controlled registers)

- EDMS,

- Hardcopy cabinet, etc.

The representatives in a typical interview list may include

- The document control team,

- The Quality compliance department,

- Engineers,

- Document Authors,

- Management team (project manager, engineering manager),

- HR,

- Contract,

- Procurement,

- Legal.

Ask open-ended questions that cannot be answered with a simple yes or no. The reason is that people tend to reveal more information when asked such questions. Investigate all possible details using queries such as,

- How do you create or modify documents?

- What are the steps?

- How do you go about reviewing and approving documents?

- Who is responsible for collecting signatures or stamps on documents?

- How do you file and retrieve documents?

- How do you register documents?

- How do you carry out a quality check on a document?

As the Interviewee responds, gather evidence by observing and inspecting samples of records. Use words like "show me" or "describe" how you do this or that to see if,

- there is evidence of control

- requirement is satisfied

- there is adequate monitoring to ensure that this level of satisfaction remains adequate and

- there is objectives and targets set monitored and met

Appendix C: Sample Document Control System Audit Report

PROCESS AUDITED: Project Document Control System	
AUDIT CRITERIA: Contract Requirements, ISO 9001: 2015 and Project Document Control Procedure, Correspondence and communication procedure.	

LEGEND/GRADE

I=Improvement
√=Conformance

NC = Non-Conformance

CAR=Corrective action request
O = Observation

ITEM#	ACTIVITY / OBSERVATION	GRADE
1.0	**Opening Meeting** The opening meeting was attended by (names) as the audit team at (specify the time)	
2.0	**Organization**	
2.1	The overall project Control organizational chart showing Document Control responsibility and authority was seen. (Document Number)	√
2.3	The Document Control team has undergone training on the Electronic Document Management system conducted by (name).	√
2.4	Evidence of training performed for	√

	a Vendor (specify vendor) document management team was seen.	
3.0	**Document Management**	
3.1	The procedures for Document Control and management have been established and approved. Some of the document seen are: • Document Numbering Procedure • Document Control Procedure • Document Control Instruction to Vendors and Subcontractors	√
3.2	Verification revealed that all project documents are being prepared with the approved project format which shows: Document Title, Document Number, Document Revision, The originator, checker and approver, and the number of pages.	√
3.3	The Master Deliverable Register (MDR) which is used for project document tracking has been established. The MDR is fully protected and updated regularly to reflect changes in document status.	√
3.4	The latest revisions of electronic and hard copies of project document were seen. A central file with proper filling arrangement is being maintained for storing project documents.	√

3.5	There was no file index for all documents stored on the file cabinet.	I
3.6	Superseded documents are suitably identified and controlled. Some of the document seen with superseded stamped are: Doc-001, Doc-005, and Doc-011	√
3.7	A well-structured and dedicated Project Share folder that provides easy access to all project documents has been established and maintained. Access to this folder is given to the project team as authorized by the Project Management.	√
3.8	Documents are issued with transmittal which is numbered sequentially in the approved project format. Hard and soft copies of signed and dated transmittals were seen. Some of the transmittals seen are: TN-001 dated dd-mm-yyyy TN-002 dated dd-mm-yyyy	√
3.9	Transmittal log, as well as query and deviation log, have been prepared and updated regularly.	√
4.0	**Vendor Document Management** Vendor document register has not been established.	O
4.1	Email workflow shows that project engineers receive documents	CAR

	directly from the Vendor contrary to the requirements in the Document Control Procedure which says that all vendor documents shall be received by the document controller for distribution to the related department.	
4.2	Vendor document Numbering and document templates are in conformance with the approved project format.	√
5.0 5.1	**Electronic Document Management System(EDMS)** A functional EDMS for controlling documents electronically has been established.	√
5.2	All canceled documents in the EDMS are clearly marked "Canceled", and indicated with a strike on the flag.	√
5.3	The reason for cancelation is not shown in the EDMS.	I
6.0	**Correspondence**	
6.1	Electronic and hard copies of correspondence (Memo and Letters) in approved project format were seen and maintained. Correspondence folders are properly numbered, labeled, and filed with an index for traceability.	√
6.2	An updated correspondence log (incoming and outgoing) has been established and it is being updated.	√

6.3	Incoming correspondence (letters) are not stamped for acknowledgment as against the requirement in the Correspondence and communication procedure. Some of the incoming letters seen without stamp are:	

Letter No	Title	Date Received
LT-010	TITLE OF LETTER_LT-010	dd-mm-yyyy
LT-015	TITLE OF LETTER_LT-015	dd-mm-yyyy
LT-021	TITLE OF LETTER_LT-021	dd-mm-yyyy

I

7.0	**<u>Recommendations</u>** 1. Document control department to modify the departmental organizational chart before the commencement of site activities to show the relationship between site and home office for effective document control management during construction activities. 2. Vendor document register should be maintained to effectively control vendor documentation. 3. File index for documents to be prepared for easy document traceability. 4. Provision to be made in the EDMS to include reasons why documents are canceled. A document Cancellation form to be established to control document cancellation process. **5.** Additional Training is required for all the EDMS on the project. It is necessary to have a trained EDMS super user amongst the document control team who will provide technical support in times of challenges. This will go a long way to improve the efficiency and effectiveness of the process.

Check Out My Other Books

Below you'll find some of my other popular books that are popular on Amazon and Kindle as well. Simply click on the links below to check them out. Alternatively, you can visit my author page on Amazon to see other work done by me.

--

https://www.amazon.com/~/e/B07H4DTR44 --

- Document Control Dictionary

- A Concise Guide on How to Select the Best Electronic Document Management System, EDMS

If the links do not work, for whatever reason, you can simply search for these titles on the Amazon website to find them.

Printed in Great Britain
by Amazon

67645254R00027